Famous American Ships

FROM THE DISCOVERY
OF THE NEW WORLD
TO THE BATTLE
OF MANILA BAY

adapted from the pages of
AMERICAN HERITAGE
The Magazine of History

by WALTER FRANKLIN

Revised Edition 1961

GOLDEN PRESS NEW YORK

Library of Congress Catalog Card Number 61-14481

The New World

From the beginning, ships have played an important part in American history. The Norsemen sailed their long narrow ships to America about 1000 A.D. Even before Columbus, Portuguese navigators may have found their way to America. A Portuguese map, dated 1424, was recently discovered in England. It shows a red rectangle, marked *Antilia,* west of the Azores. This may have been just a mistake of the map maker—or it may mean that a Portuguese navigator of the early fifteenth century reached the American mainland or a West Indian island.

Perhaps some day an old, faded chart will give proof of early voyages to the New World. But until that day comes, Columbus will be known as the discoverer of America. When he set sail with his little fleet of three ships,

This is a copy of the oldest map of the New World, drawn in 1500 by Juan de la Cosa, a shipmate of Columbus.

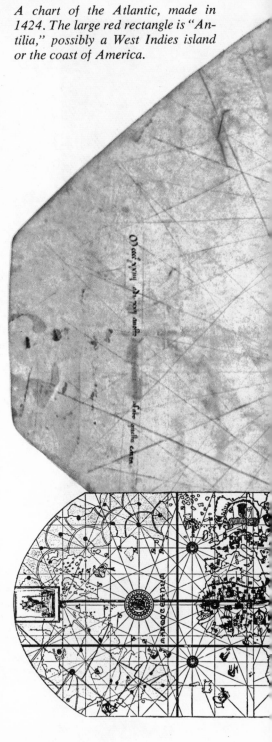

6

the Atlantic Ocean was called the Sea of Darkness and was believed to be full of strange monsters. His largest ship, the *Santa Maria,* was a merchantman with three masts. It was less than 100 feet long, weighed about 100 tons, and carried 52 men. Columbus said that it was very heavy and not suitable for the business of discovery. His other ships, the *Nina* and the *Pinta,* were smaller. The *Nina* weighed about 50 tons, the *Pinta* about the same, and each carried a crew of 18 men. They were the type of craft called caravels—a name taken from the Italian words *cara bella,* or beautiful shape.

Another early voyager was Amerigo Vespucci, who claimed to be the first man to reach North America. There are some doubts about the truth of his story, but Martin Waldseemüller, a German geographer, believed it. In

Sea monsters and flying fish surround a sailing ship of Columbus' time.

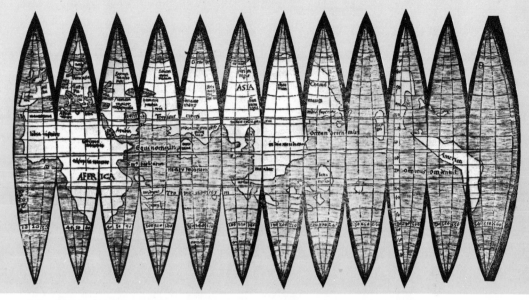

Waldseemüller's map of 1507 was pasted on a ball to form a globe of the world. This map maker was the first to name the land at the right "America."

1507 he drew up a map of the world and called the newly discovered land America, in honor of Amerigo Vespucci. It has been known by that name ever since that time.

After Columbus there were more voyages of discovery and exploration, and after the explorers came the colonists to settle in the New World—and they all came in ships. One of the most famous of the ships was the *Mayflower,* which brought the Pilgrims to New England. It sailed from England on September 16, 1620, with 102 men, women, and children crowded in dark, cramped quarters. The *Mayflower* was small and old. It weighed about 180 tons and was less than 100 feet long.

It took 55 days to reach Cape Cod, traveling 3000 miles at an average speed of two miles an hour.

The Pilgrims explored the coast in a shallop, a light open boat. Then they sailed across the bay to Plymouth harbor, where they started the first English colony in New England. During the winter they lived aboard the *Mayflower,* rowing to shore every morning to explore their new homeland, to hunt and fish and cut timber for houses. That winter was a hard one. Food was scarce, and many of the Pilgrims died. When the *Mayflower* left in April, about half of the 102 who had crossed the ocean were still alive—but not one of them returned to England.

9

At the same time that the English were settling in New England and Virginia, French expeditions under Cartier, Champlain and La Salle were pushing up the St. Lawrence River to the Great Lakes. Robert Cavelier, Sieur de la Salle, was the commander of Fort Frontenac on Lake Ontario. In November of 1678 he sent out an expedition which stopped at a place near Niagara Falls. Here, working all winter, his men built the *Griffin*, a small sailing vessel.

In August La Salle joined his men. They set sail on Lake Erie, and the *Griffin* became the first ship to travel the Great Lakes west of Lake Ontario.

Over the waters of Lake Erie, the St. Clair, Lake Huron, Lake Michigan, went the *Griffin*. La Salle dropped anchor at Green Bay to take aboard a cargo of furs. With fourteen of his men, La Salle pushed westward by canoe. The rest of his men were to take the *Griffin* back to the Niagara River, leave

A cross section of the Mayflower *shows how provisions were stored in the hold and passengers were packed into cramped quarters.*

the furs, and return to Lake Michigan. The *Griffin* set off on a stormy night — and was never heard from again. Just what happened, nobody ever knew, but she and her valuable cargo must have sunk somewhere on the lakes.

La Salle built a fort on the Illinois River, then went back to Canada. After months of hardship he started south again. It was winter and the streams were frozen, so his men put runners under the canoes and dragged them over the ice like sleds. Reaching open water, they launched their canoes and paddled down the Illinois River and into the great Mississippi. At last, in April of 1682, they reached the mouth of the mighty Mississippi. Putting up a cross and a banner, La Salle took possession of all the land he had crossed in the name of Louis, King of France, and called it Louisiana.

11

Two years later, La Salle led another expedition from France. He was to start a colony at the mouth of the Mississippi. He sailed too far west and was wrecked on the coast of Texas. He was killed by his own men after he ordered them to march to Canada, a seemingly impossible 2500 miles away.

During the same years La Salle was exploring the interior, an entirely different kind of men were exploring the hidden inlets and backwaters of the Atlantic coast. These men were pirates, who roamed the seas, attacking ships and robbing them of their cargoes. And when they wanted to stay out of sight

Amid cheering and cannon fire La Salle's Griffin *was launched on Lake Erie.*

for a while, they found the inlets and islands of the American coast a perfect place to hide.

Many of the pirates started out as privateers. A privateer was a sea captain who had "letters of marque" from his government, allowing him to capture enemy ships. His reward was a share of the loot. Sir Francis Drake, for example, held letters of marque from Queen Elizabeth of England. He captured Spanish ships, and in 1585 he even attacked the Spanish colony of Santo Domingo, in what is today the Dominican Republic.

Often, when enemy ships were scarce, privateers became pirates. They attacked the ships of all nations, including their own. By the end of the 17th century, many pirates were using the hiding places along the North American coast. One of the most famous pirates was Blackbeard.

Blackbeard's real name was Edward Teach. He was given his nickname be-

cause of his long, black whiskers, which, "like a frightful meteor, covered his whole face." Blackbeard did everything he could to look as fierce as possible. He carried six pistols in his scarlet silk sash and sometimes held a two-foot knife between his teeth. Before going into battle, he would stick lighted matches under the brim of his hat to give himself a terrifying aspect.

Blackbeard's favorite hiding places were along the coast of North Carolina, and he shared his loot with North Carolina's governor. But at last, in 1718, the governor of Virginia sent out Lieutenant Robert Maynard, with orders to capture Blackbeard. As Maynard's ship came close, Blackbeard drank a toast and roared, "I'll give no quarter nor take any from you!"

Blackbeard's cannon fired, then he and fourteen of his men leaped to the deck of Maynard's ship. Blackbeard was killed in the battle. His head was cut off and carried ashore and set up

This pictorial map shows the ships of privateer Sir Francis Drake in the harbor of Santo Domingo, now Ciudad Trujillo in the Dominican Republic.

named the *Bonhomme Richard*. With three other ships, Jones set off in his ancient ship to search for the enemy.

On the night of September 23, Jones sighted a fleet of 39 British merchant ships led by two men-of-war, the *Serapis* and the *Countess of Scarborough*. The *Bonhomme Richard* and the *Serapis* fired their cannon at each other, and one of the greatest naval battles in history began. For hours, by the light of the moon, the fight went on. About half of Jones' crew were killed or wounded. His ship was on fire and starting to sink. The flagstaff snapped, the flag fell into the water, and a cheer went up from the *Serapis*. The British captain called out to Jones, asking him if he surrendered.

"Surrender?" shouted Jones. "I have just begun to fight!"

The two ships were now side by side, and Jones ordered some of his crew to board the *Serapis*. They leaped to the deck of the British vessel, and there was hand-to-hand fighting. Meanwhile, Jones' snipers were firing their muskets, bringing down the British gunners. Then an American grenade struck the store of powder on the *Serapis*. The explosion wrecked her starboard guns and brought the mainmast crashing down. Soon, at thirty-five minutes past ten, the British surrendered. But the *Bonhomme Richard* could not stay afloat for long, and the next morning

on a pole at Hampton, Virginia. Not long after Blackbeard's death, piracy gradually died out on the coast of the American colonies.

As the years passed, ships continued to play an important part in American history. The Boston Tea Party, which helped bring on the American Revolution, took place on a British merchant ship in Boston harbor. When the Revolution itself started, the Americans had no navy and began building ships. But ships of war remained scarce. Even in 1779, Captain John Paul Jones had to sail on a battered French merchantman. It was repaired, refitted, and re-

16

Jones transferred his crew to the *Serapis*. He stood on deck, watching sadly as the *Bonhomme Richard* slid under the waves to the bottom of the sea.

After the United States won its independence, it went on building up a navy. Its ships were frigates—small, fast vessels with 20 to 50 guns—rather than the heavier type, called ships of the line, which carried at least 60 guns. Most famous of the frigates was the *Constitution*. She was built in 1797, of

Captain Bartholomew Roberts was one of the most famous pirates of the 18th century. In a remarkable demonstration of seamanship, he once captured eleven ships with only two of his own.

The Bonhomme Richard *fought the British* Serapis *in a great naval battle.*

The Constitution, *nicknamed "Old Ironsides," battled the* Guerrière.

In another naval battle in 1812, Stephen Decatur, captain of the United States, *captured the British ship* Macedonian *with little damage. He brought his valuable prize back to New York.*

In 1812 the Constitution *and the British frigate* Java *met in battle off Brazil.*

live oak and red cedar, and her bolts, spikes and bell were made by Paul Revere. She carried 51 guns and a crew of about 450 men.

During the first year of the War of 1812, the *Constitution* met the British ship *Guerrière* off Halifax, 600 miles east of Boston. Captain Isaac Hull, the American commander, held his fire until he brought his vessel close to the enemy. Then the two ships blasted away at each other. Cannon balls seemed to bounce off the *Constitution's* sides, and her crew gave her the nickname of "Old Ironsides." But the *Guerrière* did not stand up so well. Her hull was ripped, her masts were shattered, and 78 of her sailors were killed or wounded. After thirty minutes of battle, the British surrendered.

Several months later, the *Constitution* sank the British frigate *Java* off

The Constitution *shot down the* Java's *masts, leaving the British ship helpless.*

The British surrendered and their crew was removed from the Java.

Brazil. The world was amazed by the victories of the young American nation over the finest navy on the seas, and the feats of the *Constitution* will always be remembered.

By 1830 the great frigate was old and useless, and the Navy ordered her scrapped. But Oliver Wendell Holmes' poem, *Old Ironsides*, stirred Americans everywhere. They refused to let her be destroyed, and she was rebuilt in 1833.

In 1855 she was used as a training ship in the Portsmouth navy yard. She was rebuilt again in 1877 and in 1925, and today she can still be seen, anchored in Boston harbor.

Other ships of the War of 1812 won fame without even going to sea. They did their fighting on inland waters. In 1813 Commodore Oliver Hazard Perry led a small fleet against a squadron of British vessels in Lake Erie. After his

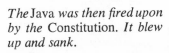

The Java *was then fired upon by the* Constitution. *It blew up and sank.*

During the War of 1812, the British frigate Shannon *captured the American ship* Chesapeake *after fifteen minutes of fighting.*

Salem merchants traded with the Orient in square-rigged ships.

own ship, the *Lawrence,* was wrecked, he transferred to the *Niagara* and won the battle. Then he sent a message to General William Henry Harrison: "We have met the enemy and they are ours; two ships, two brigs, one schooner and one sloop."

About a year later, Captain William Macdonough won an important victory on Lake Champlain. He defeated an English fleet larger than his own in two hours and twenty minutes.

The merchant ships of America were just as famous as its fighters. Immediately after the Revolution, American craft sailed to ports scattered everywhere on the globe. Baltimore topsail schooners, with sharp bows and narrow hulls, went up and down the coast. Barks and brigs, with large square sails and triangular fore-and-aft sails, voyaged across the ocean.

Trade with China began after Samuel Shaw gave a report of his voyage to Canton. The *Grand Turk,* whose home port was Salem, Massachusetts, was the first New England ship that reached China. She was soon followed by ships from Boston, Providence, Philadelphia and New York. The Chinese set up

24

Salem's ships sometimes met disaster in stormy weather. The ship Ulysses *and two others were wrecked on the shores of Cape Cod, with a loss of eighty-seven lives.*

Hongs, or special trading stations for foreigners, along the water front at Canton. Here American sea captains traded for tea, spices, silk, ivory, chinaware, and other goods of the Orient which brought high prices back at home.

Then Salem sent its ships to Africa and the East Indies to bring back coffee, pepper, silks, ivory and gold. Although Salem was only a small town, its sea captains became known throughout the world, and its merchants were among the richest in the United States. Their warehouses were crammed full of the treasures of the East, and in their fine houses on Chestnut Street were many rare and beautiful souvenirs of strange and distant lands.

Flags of western countries flew at the Hongs, or trading posts, on the Canton water front.

Ships dock at a Salem wharf in the days when the city was a great port for world trade.

Salem's captains and seamen brought home many rare and interesting things, such as a goblet carved from the horn of a rhinoceros or the tooth of an elephant. One captain brought back a live elephant, the first ever seen in America. It cost him $450.

Salem remained a great port until the 1820's and '30's, when American shipyards began turning out bigger ships. They were too big for Salem's shallow harbor, and the merchants began losing business to Boston, which had deeper waters in its harbor. Year by year, the warehouses and the wharves were closed. At last, except for the mansions on Chestnut Street, little was left of the great days of Salem shipping.

Meanwhile, ships sailing from other American ports were still making history. The Black Ball Line of New York, begun in 1818, was running regular scheduled voyages to and from England. Packets, as any ships which ran on a regular schedule were called, were something new. Before this, ships would delay sailing because of the weather, or for want of passengers or freight. More packet lines, such as the Red Star and the Swallowtail, were started and helped make New York City the greatest seaport in the United States.

At the same time that packets were crossing the Atlantic, American merchant ships were sailing all over the globe. New England lads who had seen little of their own country were at home in the ports of China, the South Seas, and the Indies. Their ship's cargo might contain tar, flour, tobacco, butter, iron, sugar, chocolate, brandy, beef, and candles. One of the strangest cargoes was New England ice, which was packed in sawdust and sent to the hot lands of India, the West Indies and South America. Some ships carried live cargo, bringing slaves from Africa to the West Indies and America.

American whaling ships roamed the oceans, from the Arctic to the South Seas, on voyages that often lasted as long as three years. For America needed whale oil for its lamps, and there were whales to be caught in the deep waters of the world. Among the first to go whaling were the men of Nantucket. Whaling became Nantucket's business, and even the men who stayed ashore made a living from whaling, as ropemakers, sailmakers, or blacksmiths. Other ports also sent out whalers, but Nantucket led them all until the 1840's. Then larger whaling ships were built — too large for the waters around Nan-

Merchants flew their own flags over their warehouses and on their ships. These flags were known in China, India and throughout the East Indies.

Whaling ships roamed the oceans for many years at a time.

tucket. New Bedford had a deeper harbor and soon was the leading port for whalers. By 1857 it was the home port for 329 whaling ships, the largest fleet of whalers in the world.

Whaling ships were much like merchant ships. They were not built for speed, but for work—the work of killing giant whales, cutting up the blubber and boiling it down into oil. Most whaling ships had three masts. High on the foremast and the mainmast stood the lookouts, watching for signs of whales. As soon as they spied the spout of a whale in the water, they cried out: "Blows! There she blows!"

Sometimes weeks or even months would go by before a whale was sighted. The crew would pass the time by doing scrimshaw work—carving things from whale's teeth and jawbones, and cutting designs and pictures into them. Sometimes two whaling ships would meet each other, and they would have a "gam." Captains and crews would visit, exchanging news and gossip. After the gam, the two ships would sail on,

This scrimshaw is engraved with a ship.

When whales were sighted, small boats were lowered for the chase.

searching the waters for whales. Sooner or later, the cry would come from the lookout: "There she blows!" Then the chase began.

Whaleboats were 30 feet long, weighed between five and six hundred pounds, and carried a crew of six. Over the waves, after the whale, they rowed. When they were close enough, the harpooner stood up in the bow. He hurled his harpoon, a sort of a long iron spear attached to the boat by a long line. When the sharp point sank in, the whale swam furiously, thrashed about, and dived under the water. The long rope attached to the harpoon held the whale near the boat. As the whale rushed across the water, it pulled the boat after it in a wild, dangerous "Nantucket sleigh ride."

Often the whale would lash out with its tail, upsetting the boat and sending the crew to its death. But if all went well, the great beast of the sea would at last grow tired. One of the crew would plunge a lance into the whale for the kill and the chase was ended.

This scrimshaw pictures a country scene.

The harpooners stand ready to attack the whale.

After the whale died, it was tied to the side of the ship, which now became a sort of floating factory. The blubber, or fat, was stripped from the carcass, cut up into pieces, and boiled in big try-pots until it was melted into oil. Black smoke rose from the pots, and the ship was filled with a foul smell. Day and night the pots bubbled, boiling down tons of blubber. The oil was poured into barrels, which were placed in the hold. Besides ordinary whale oil, sperm oil would be taken from the head of a sperm whale. It was used for lubricating watches, sewing machines, and other fine machinery. Whalebone was also saved. And, if the crew was lucky, it would find a lump of ambergris—a substance which forms in the stomach of a sick whale. Ambergris was used in the making of perfume and was worth as much as four hundred dollars a pound.

After everything was stowed away and the decks washed, the whaling ship sailed on. Again it was scrimshaw, and watch and wait, watch and wait, until the lookout cried: "Blows! There she blows!" Then there was another chase, another whale, and more blubber to boil. And so it went, with the ship cruising the vast and lonely waters of the earth, making for home only when every barrel aboard was full of oil.

But while the captains of whaling vessels thought little about speed, the captains in the China tea trade thought of nothing else. Tea kept too long in the hold of a ship lost its flavor, and the merchants of London were willing to pay well for fast delivery. And so American shipbuilders began turning out clippers—and clippers were made for speed.

The clippers had slender, streamlined, round-bottomed hulls, with sharp bows and rounded sterns. They were much more graceful than the merchant and whaling ships, which had blunt bows and square sterns. And the clippers used much more sail. Their three towering masts carried a cloud of sail—a mainsail, topsails, topgallants, royals, skysails, and moonrakers.

When the Gold Rush of 1849 began, thousands of men wanted to get from the East Coast to California. Many of them went by land, but just as many went by sea, from New York and Boston around Cape Horn. And they went on clippers. A few years later there was a gold rush in Australia. Again the

A thrashing whale could easily overturn a whaleboat.

A cartoon makes fun of the mania for speed during the Gold Rush to California.

prospectors went on clippers, sailing from England. For the clippers were the fastest sailing vessels afloat, and they broke record after record. The *Flying Cloud* sailed 433 miles in one day and took only 89 days to reach San Francisco from New York. The *Sovereign of the Seas* once made 5200 miles in three weeks. The *Lightning* crossed the Atlantic, from New York to Liverpool, in 13 days, 19½ hours. One day in 1854, her captain wrote in

The clipper Lightning *was one of the fastest sailing vessels ever built.*

the logbook: "Wind South, strong gales ...distance run in 24 hours 436 miles."

With their trim lines and clouds of sail, clippers were as beautiful as they were swift. But for the seamen who had to work on them, life was hard. A sailor had to be strong and agile. Captains called for speed, speed, and more speed, and drove their crews without mercy. Captain Waterman of the *Sea Witch* was even known to shoot men for handling the sails too slowly to suit him. Clippers needed large crews, and wages were small — about eight dollars a month.

33

The clipper Zephyr *sails into the harbor at Messina, Sicily, in 1860.*

The great days of the clippers lasted only from 1846 to 1859. For one thing, their holds were too small to carry much cargo. Operating costs were high. But it was steam that really put them out of business.

The first American crossing of the Atlantic with the help of steam took place in 1819. The American ship *Savannah*, a sailing vessel fitted with steam engines and paddlewheels sailed from Savannah, Georgia, to Liverpool, England, in 27 days, or 648 hours. Her wood-burning engines were operated for a total of only 80 hours. But by 1850 steamers were making the New York-Liverpool crossing in less than 11 days. Slowly, one by one, the proud sailing vessels were pushed off the seas and left to rot.

Fighting ships, too, were changing. The United States Navy experimented with two steam vessels, the *Fulton I*, which blew up in 1829, and the *Fulton II*. In 1840 Commodore Matthew Calbraith Perry put through his plan for a steam frigate. She had three masts and carried sails for emergencies. Named the *Mississippi*, she served as Perry's flagship in the Mexican War. She went with Perry to the Pacific when he made the first treaty between the United States and Japan, and later went around the world.

The *Mississippi* was built of wood, and so were the other Navy ships built after her. Then, during the Civil War, something happened that decided the future of wooden fighting ships forever.

On the morning of March 8, 1862, a strange Confederate craft came steaming toward the Union fleet at Hampton Roads. She was the *Merrimac*, perhaps the first ironclad warship in history. She had begun life as a Union frigate, and had been left behind when the Union forces retreated from the Norfolk Navy Yard. The Confederate Navy rebuilt her, constructing a sort of shed on the deck. The sides of this shed were covered with heavy iron plates. She carried ten guns, fired through ports protected by big iron lids. With a noise like thunder, the Union guns opened fire. The cannon balls struck the *Merrimac's* iron sides—and bounced off. On and on she came, toward the Union frigate *Cumberland*, taking broadside after broadside from the Union ship.

The Arctic, one of the first American packets to use steam in transatlantic crossings, was struck by a French steamer in foggy weather. She sank off the coast of Newfoundland.

From a window of Fort Monroe, a telegraph operator—a boy of fourteen—watched the *Merrimac* as she steamed in to battle. He sent this message over the wire:

"She is steering straight for the *Cumberland* ... the *Cumberland* gives her a broadside ... she keels over ... seems to be sinking ... she comes in again ... she has struck the *Cumberland* and poured a broadside into her ... God! the *Cumberland* is sinking ..."

After ramming the *Cumberland*, the *Merrimac* attacked the *Congress*, setting her afire. By this time her coal and ammunition were low, and she

The first battle of ironclad ships was fought in the Civil War between the Union Monitor *and the Confederate* Merrimac *at Hampton Roads, Virginia. The battle lasted four hours.*

steamed away. The Union commander knew she would be back, and that she would try to finish off his entire fleet. But the next day, on March ninth, came the Union's answer to the *Merrimac*. It was the *Monitor*, an even stranger ironclad craft which had steamed all the way from New York.

For months inventor John Ericsson had been at work in New York, building the Union a new type of ship. The hull was almost all below the waterline. On her deck was a round turret for the guns. There were only two guns, but the turret could be rotated, so that the guns could fire in any direction.

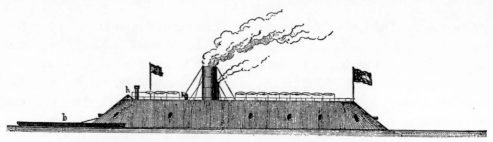

The Merrimac *was covered with iron plates four inches thick.*

For hours the two ironclads fought. They touched each other five times, once when the *Merrimac* tried to ram the Union ship with her iron prow. A shot struck the *Monitor's* pilothouse, and her captain was blinded by gunpowder. He turned his command over to young Lieutenant S. Dana Greene. Neither ship could do any real damage to the other, and at last the *Merrimac* retreated. But the *Monitor* had saved the fleet of wooden frigates, and her crew believed they had won a victory.

"The fight was over now, and we were victorious," Lieutenant Greene wrote a few days later in a letter to his family. "My men and myself were perfectly black with smoke and powder . . ." The Assistant Secretary of the Navy, who was on the frigate *Minnesota,* hailed them and said that they "had fought the greatest naval battle on record, and behaved as gallantly as men could."

The two ships never met again. Two months later, when the Confederates had to give up the Norfolk Navy Yard, the *Merrimac* was destroyed by its own crew. And on December 31 of that same year, the *Monitor* was sunk in a storm off Cape Hatteras. But the world already knew that wooden fighting ships would never be built again.

And so, in the navies as well as the merchant fleets that traveled the seas, wood and sail gave way to iron and steam. On the rivers of America, too, things had changed. Boats were still made of wood—but they were powered by steam. In fact, steam was used on rivers long before it was used at sea. As early as 1786, John Fitch built a

A cutaway view of the Monitor *shows her revolving gun turret, the first in history.*

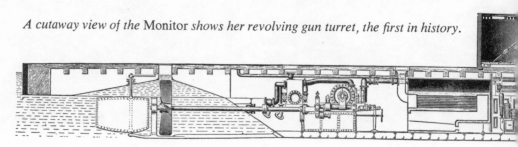

Robert Fulton's Clermont *was the first successful American steamboat.*

craft with paddles driven by steam. Other inventors experimented with similar devices, and in 1807 America's first practical steamboat went up the Hudson River. It was Robert Fulton's *Clermont,* which was 150 feet long and had a speed of five miles an hour. It made regular trips between New York City and Albany and was soon earning money for its owners.

There were many rivers in America, and travel by water had long been an important way of moving goods or getting places. Canoes, rafts, flatboats, keelboats—all these were in use. It was easy enough to float them downstream. But pushing upstream was hard, slow work, and often impossible. No wonder, then, that Americans welcomed the steamboat, which could go upstream as well as down. Within twenty years of the *Clermont's* first trip, steamboats were chugging on the Mississippi, the Missouri, and other western rivers. The cry of "Steamboat a-comin'!" was heard in hundreds of river towns. And in the 1850's and '60's came the great

days of the Mississippi steamboat. New Orleans became one of the busiest ports in the country, with boats to and from St. Louis, Pittsburgh, Cincinnati, Louisville, Vicksburg, Nashville, Memphis, Florence, Shreveport, Natchez, and Jefferson City.

The boats were so big and fancy that they were called floating palaces. Over a low hull like a flatboat's rose two or three decks, topped by a pilot house and two tall smokestacks. Freight and wood for fuel were carried on the lower deck, near the engines that turned the paddlewheels. On the upper decks were staterooms for sleeping and a large cabin for dining. The cabin had wooden pillars, painted

The turret was protected by 8-inch armor.

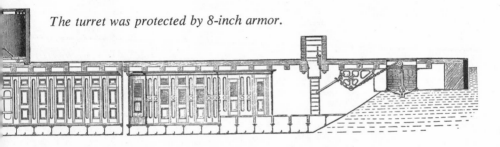

Steam-driven paddle-wheeled river boats made transportation faster.

white and gilt, and carved wooden brackets. On the floor were thick carpets; on the walls were paintings and draperies. By day the light came through stained glass windows; by night from crystal chandeliers. Here, the passengers ate fine meals, lounged on plush-covered sofas, or enjoyed music, dancing, and cardplaying.

Passengers on a river boat had a good time—unless there was an acci-dent. Many boats were destroyed by hitting snags—logs sticking up from the river bottom—by collisions, by fire, and, worst of all, by boiler explosions. By 1850, about 185 boats had blown up, killing more than 1400 persons. The most terrible accident in the history of steamboats took place in April, 1865. At least 2300 men, most of them Union soldiers returning home, had crowded on the *Sultana,* a boat meant to carry no more than 400. She was just above Memphis, at two in the morning, when the boilers exploded.

A stern-wheeler and a side-wheeler steam along the Mississippi.

About 1700 men were killed, many by burning or drowning.

In spite of the dangers, steamboat captains and pilots tried for greater and greater speed. Often two boats going in the same direction would race against each other. Sometimes a race would be arranged in advance, like the famous one between the *Natchez* and the *Robert E. Lee.* Both boats were well known, and so were their captains. Word of the race spread, and crowds gathered on shore to see the start. On June 30, 1870, the boats set out from New Orleans for St. Louis, 1200 miles away. Captain John W. Cannon of the *Robert E. Lee* took no chances. He carried no freight and stripped his boat of all extra weight. Captain Thomas P. Leathers of the *Natchez* was so sure of winning that he took on a load of freight and planned to make all regular stops.

The *Robert E. Lee* was the first to

Some of the early steamboats blew up when overheated boilers exploded.

Awful Conflagration of the Steam boat **LEXINGTON** In Long Island Sound on Monday Eve?, Jan? 13th 1840. by which melancholy occurrence; over 100 PERSONS PERISHED.

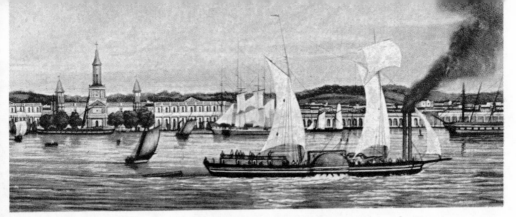

An early steamboat with sails passes along the New Orleans levee.

get away. The *Natchez* followed in four minutes. Within 24 hours the *Robert E. Lee* was at Vicksburg; the *Natchez* was 16 minutes behind. At Memphis the *Natchez* was an hour behind. Then, at Cairo, Illinois, the *Natchez* ran aground. She was delayed by fog and could not possibly win. The *Robert E. Lee* went on at full speed, reaching St. Louis in three days, 18 hours and 13 minutes—a record which still stands.

Captain Leathers refused to admit that the *Robert E. Lee* was the faster

The Robert E. Lee *beat the* Natchez *in a race up the Mississippi from New Orleans to St. Louis. The entire population of towns along the river came out to cheer them on.*

*Flat-bottomed river boats could travel in the shallow waters
of the bayou country without fear of running aground.*

boat. He said that if he had not been delayed six hours by the fog and 36 minutes repairing a pump, he would have won by 20 minutes. Captain Leathers lived until he was 80 years old, when he was knocked down by a "scorcher," a speeding bicyclist. He died of his injuries in 1896—still believing that the *Natchez* should have won the race.

The steamboats on the western rivers were built with flat bottoms so that they could be used in shallow waters.

Some captains boasted that their boats could run on a heavy dew. In the East, a somewhat different type of steamboat, one with a deeper hull, was used on the Hudson River and along the Atlantic Coast.

Regular steamboat service on the Long Island Sound began in 1847, when the *Firefly* started running between Newport and Providence, Rhode Island. Masters of sailing vessels made fun of the smoky little steamer, and offered to carry their passengers free if they could not beat her. No one had much faith in steam. After several prominent men refused a ride up the Sound in the *Firefly,* her owner gave up the business.

Five years later, however, steamboat service came to the Sound to stay. Steamboats were bigger, more dependable, more luxurious. A number of lines operated from New York City. The best known was the Fall River Line, which ran boats along Long Island Sound, past Newport, to Fall River. Here passengers could catch the train to Boston.

By 1869 the Fall River Line was owned by Jim Fisk, a well-known financier. Two of his boats, the *Bristol* and the *Providence,* could each carry more than 800 passengers. Fisk decorated them with fine fixtures, and in each boat he placed 250 canaries in cages.

Like the boats on the Mississippi, the boats on the Hudson and Long Island Sound were floating palaces. The *Commonwealth* and the *Priscilla* were elegantly furnished. They had bands to make music for the passengers, and carpets on the floors. The

Passengers relax in the luxurious grand cabin of a boat of the Fall River Line.

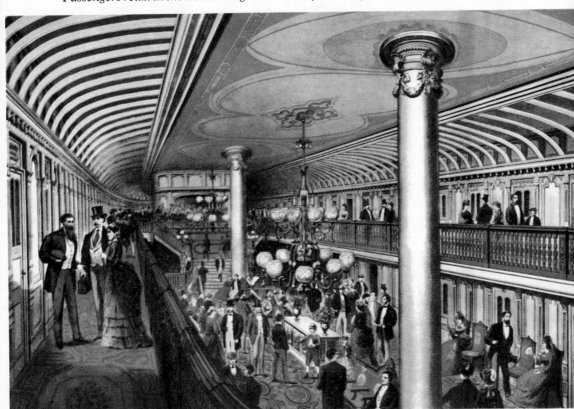

This scene shows the flagship Priscilla *and two other steamers of the Fall River Line.*

Pilgrim had room for 1200 persons and was advertised as being lighted with "1000 incandescent electric lights." The Fall River Line was known throughout the country. Many famous people, including presidents of the United States, traveled on it at one time or another. There were even songs written about the old Fall River. And the boats were as safe as they were comfortable. In 90 years the line lost only one passenger.

The East had a famous race, too, between George Law's *Oregon* and Commodore Vanderbilt's *C. Vanderbilt,* named after himself. Thousands

These were the fastest passenger ships in the East coast trade.

of people cheered as the two boats steamed away from the Battery in New York City on a fine spring morning in 1847. The course of the race was up the Hudson to Ossining, then back again, for a prize of $1000.

The boats were even until they reached the turning point at Ossining, where they ran into each other. Neither boat was badly damaged. But the pilot of the *C. Vanderbilt* became confused, and the *Oregon* took the lead. Near Yonkers, the *Oregon* ran out of fuel. Chairs, benches, berths, doors, expensive paneling were tossed into the fire. They kept the *Oregon* going,

49

The explosion of the Maine *helped bring on the Spanish-American War.*

and she reached the finish line first, only a few lengths in front.

In the East and in the West, steamboating began to die out in the late 1800's. The Fall River Line lasted longer than most of the coastal lines but in 1937 it, too, gave up. And it was steam that drove the floating palaces off the rivers—steam that powered the locomotives of the railroads that criss-crossed the United States. Trains were faster, cheaper, more convenient, and travelers preferred them to boats.

As the floating palaces disappeared from the rivers, American naval vessels were making history at sea. After the battle of the *Monitor* and the *Merrimac*, Britain had taken the lead in developing armored fighting ships. For many years the United States did little, but by the 1880's it began building up its navy. One of the new ships was the battleship *Maine*.

The *Maine* was 324.3 feet long and could make a speed as high as 17 knots. She carried four 12-inch guns, six 6-inch guns, seven 6-pounders, and twelve smaller guns.

On February 15, 1898, the *Maine* was lying at anchor in Havana Harbor, Cuba, which was then under the rule of Spain. Cuba was in the midst of a revolution, and the *Maine* was sent down to protect American interests in the country. That night, at twenty minutes to ten, the *Maine* blew up with a terrific explosion. Of the 354 men aboard, 260 were killed and 47

50

RECOVERING THE DEAD BODIES.

injured. Exactly what caused the explosion was never learned, although official investigators found that mines had been discharged underneath the ship's magazines, blowing up the explosives stored in the ship's hold.

American sympathy was on the side of the Cuban revolution and they put the blame on Spain. "Remember the *Maine!*" Americans cried—and by April the United States and Spain were at war. A squadron of ships under the command of Commodore George Dewey at Hong Kong sailed for the Philippines, Spain's Pacific possession. Within ten days they reached Manila Bay. On the clear, calm night of April 30, Dewey sailed into the heavily guarded and mined bay. Ignoring the fire from the city, he sailed to within 5,000 yards of the Spanish fleet which was waiting at anchor in battle formation. Dewey then gave the order: "You may fire when ready, Gridley." And in two hours eleven Spanish ships were destroyed—without the loss of a single American life! Several weeks later, the rest of the Spanish fleet was destroyed at Santiago Harbor, Cuba. Meanwhile, the American army was winning victories on land, and in 82 days the war was over.

Once again ships had played an important part in American history. The earliest ships had brought the discoverers and explorers over an unknown ocean to an unknown land. In canoes and rafts and small craft they adventured inland on the rivers and lakes of the New World. They were followed by settlers, who built their homes on the eastern shore. Many died on the dangerous voyage. Still they came, in ship after ship, from country after country in the Old World.

And when they had settled on the land, they built ships of their own, and went sailing to far ports. They fought to found a new nation, the United States of America, and some of the fighting was done in ships. After the fighting was over, they sailed even farther. They sailed for trade and they sailed for whales, on the seven seas of the world. Yankee inventors tinkered with steam, until steamboats chugged up and down all the rivers. As the nation grew, steamboats carried settlers to the West. The clippers, the last of the sailing vessels, carried men to California and goods to and from the Orient. Sail gave way to steam, on the oceans as well as on the rivers. Iron replaced wood as Americans fought to preserve their nation undivided.

All this was in the past when the American navy won its victory over the Spanish fleet. Ahead were the swift passenger liners, the sturdy freighters of peacetime and the ships which would explore new frontiers beneath the polar icecap and at the bottom of the oceans; the battleships, aircraft carriers and submarines of war. And there would be more to come. For America was a land of lakes and rivers, bounded by two great oceans, and ships would always be a part of its history.

Commodore Dewey stands on the bridge of his ship, the Olympia, *on the morning of the battle of Manila Bay.*

52

PICTURE CREDITS